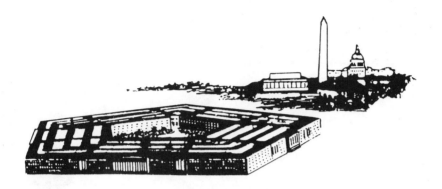

PENTAGON TIDBITS

by Nita Scoggan

D1712225

ROYALTY PUBLISHING COMPANY

P.O. Box 2016   Manassas, Virginia, 22110

A Nation's Greatness

Ralph Waldo Emerson

Not gold, but only man can make
   A people great and strong;
Men who for truth and honor's sake,
   Stand fast and suffer long.

Brave men who work while others sleep
   Who dare while others fly . . .
They build a nation's pillars deep
   And lift them to the sky.

ROYALTY PUBLISHING COMPANY
P.O. Box 2016
Manassas, VA 22110

Scenes of the Pentagon reproduced from original watercolor
paintings by Nita Scoggan.
Inspirational painting by Woodi Ishmael, page 29, USAF Art Collection

ISBN 0-910487-30-8
Library of Congress Catalog Number: 93-087336

THE PENTAGON

Headquarters of our nation's
Department of Defense
is
The World's Largest Office Building

THEIR WORK

Charged by the U.S. Constitution to:
"Insure domestic tranquility, Provide for the Common
defense, Promote the general welfare, and secure the Blessings
of Liberty to ourselves and our Posterity..."

Construction – Wartime Miracle

The Pentagon was designed and built in a race against time. It was planned for efficiency, not beauty. Frills and non–functional items were omitted wherever possible. Passenger elevator service was eliminated due to wartime economy.

During the early part of 1941, the President asked Congress for a building to be constructed in or near the District of Columbia, to house the combined military leaders and better coordinate their functions.

Construction began on September 11, 1941, on a 24–hour a day schedule. At one stage, 15,000 men were employed on the job. Work was completed at record speed. Under normal conditions, construction of such a building would take a total of four years. Although constructed in swampy area known as "Hell's Bottom," the Pentagon has held up well, thanks to the structural frame of steel and reinforced concrete, supported by the 41,192 concrete piles on which it rests.

The first office workers began to move in on April 29, 1942, while some construction work was still in progress. There are no escalators to the fifth floor, since there were only four floors in the original design. All construction was completed by January 15, 1943, at a cost of about $83,000,000.

With unification of the Armed Services in 1947, the Pentagon became headquarters for the entire military. Originally designated as the National Military Establishment, the Pentagon later became the Department of Defense.

In the late 1970s an incinerator was installed on the Heating Plant site adjacent to the Pentagon. This incinerator burns nonpulpable classified materials formerly burned elsewhere. Almost 25% of the Pentagon's steam for generating heat and hot water is produced here. About 10 tons of classified waste is burned daily. For every two tons of material burned, one ton of coal is saved.

Pentagon building site -- a swamp!

The Amazing Structure

Few people throughout the world have not heard of the Pentagon. However, a relatively small number have had the opportunity to tour the building which is the center of our national defense.

The Pentagon covers 34 acres. The five–sided, five–storied building is located near the Potomac River, opposite the Nation's Capital, in Arlington, Virginia. The fortress–like, five–sided shape makes the building unique. Each of the five outside walls is 921 feet in length, so the distance around the outer ring of the building is almost a mile! The building is faced with Indiana limestone.

The cavernous Pentagon has three times the floor space of the 102–floor Empire State Building in New York city and is twice the size of the Merchandise Mart in Chicago. The U.S. Capitol building could fit into any one of its five wedge–shaped sections, which total about 6,500,000 square feet of floor space.

The River Entrance and The Mall Entrance are located on the two sides of the building which face Washington, D.C. The River Entrance overlooks an attractive lagoon which provides access by water, and mooring for small pleasure craft nearby. The Concourse entrance is accessed by the Metro or from South Parking area.

The building was limited to five stories above ground due to its proximity to National Airport, so that the structure would not pose a hazard to planes using one of the nation's busiest airports.

The Pentagon's five–acre center court provides a park–like atmosphere for employees to eat their lunch or stretch their legs.

The wide ramps between floors are a unique feature of the building. These ramps would be particularly useful in case of emergencies, when it might be necessary to clear the thousands of workers rapidly. Despite the vastness of the Pentagon, no two offices are more than 1,800 feet apart––about a ten minute walk.

Variety of foods & seating for 4,000 in the six cafeterias

Pentagon's five-acre center court

Points of Interest

The Navy, Air Force, Army and Marine Executive Corridors, the Hall of Heroes, Eisenhower, War Correspondents, Military Women, and the Constitution Corridors feature historical events, models of the latest planes, ships and military trophies.

The Commander-in-Chief's Corridor portrays significant military events and a brief biography of each President. Facts such as: * Franklin Roosevelt served the longest term in office – twelve years. * William Harrison served the shortest term in office – died after one month. * Abraham Lincoln was our tallest President – 6 feet 4 inches. * James Buchanan was our only bachelor.

In the Flag Corridor, colorful flags from every state are displayed. Tour guides explain interesting facts, such as: "The Rattlesnake Flag almost became our national flag! The rattles to warn the enemy--if ignored it would strike with deadly force."

The Berlin Wall exhibit features a large remnant of the Wall, presented as a testament to the constant vigil maintained by the men and women of the U.S. Army along German borders since the end of World War II. The Wall, erected in 1961 as a barrier to keep East German citizens from fleeing to the West, was torn down in November 1989, by people set free from Communism.

The "Iron Curtain" Exhibit features many of the original parts of the barrier--the barbed wire, guard towers, electronic tripwires and minefields which separated Hungary from the west. Erected in 1956, the "Iron Curtain" was taken down by Hungarians in 1989. Secretary of Defense Dick Cheney opened the exhibit March 17, 1992. It was given by the Hungarians to commemorate the reunification of Europe.

The Pentagon celebrated its 50th anniversary in 1993. It honored those who worked here--unsung heroes--guarding our Nation by performing 24-hour a day, year around vital functions.

Heliport

Nita Scoggan

Hall of Heroes

On the archway leading to the Hall of Heroes is the motto of West Point and General MacArthur: DUTY–HONOR–COUNTRY.

The Medal of Honor is the highest military award. It is given out for an act of bravery above and beyond the call of duty. The deed must be proved beyond any doubt by testimony of at least two eye witnesses; it must be so outstanding that it shows acts beyond the call of duty, and must involve the risk of life.

In 1991, President Bush presented the Medal of Honor to Georgia Palmer and Mary Bowens from Greenville, SC on behalf of their brother, Cpl. Freddie Stowers, for action during WWI. He is the only black American to receive the Medal of Honor in WWI.

For acts of bravery during the 1968 Vietnam Conflict MSgt.Roy Benavidez was awarded this Medal by President Reagan.

The Medal of Honor is normally awarded only during wartime, but Congress has on rare occasions, awarded Medals of Honor for deeds taking place in peacetime. The Medal is presented by the President in the name of Congress, which is why it is sometimes called the Congressional Medal of Honor.

There are over 3,400 recipients of this medal. The most highly decorated soldier during WWII to include the Medal of Honor was Audie Murphy. The first Air Force recipient was Capt. Eddie Richenbacker, ace of aces, he shot down 26 planes.

Dr. Mary E. Walker is the only female recipient of the Medal of Honor. She was not a commissioned officer in the military, but was a contract surgeon during the Civil War. She risked her life going to the front lines to help wounded soldiers. She was a prisoner of war for four months in a southern prison. Upon the recommendation of Major Generals Sherman and Thomas, President Andrew Johnson ordered the medal be given on November 11, 1865.

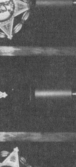

HALL OF HEROES

HALL OF HEROES

HALL OF HEROES

Military Women's Corridor

This corridor features a fine collection of historical memorabilia and 80 photographs pertaining to the contribution of women to the defense of the nation.

One case highlights Dr. Mary E. Walker, the only female Medal of Honor recipient. As a contract surgeon, she risked her life helping wounded soldiers on the front lines during the Civil War.

During WW I, women were allowed to enlist for the first time in the Navy, Marines and Coast Guard. The Army hired women as civilians under contract until WWII, when they were able to enlist.

One display features Grace Hopper, who at age 79 retired as a Rear Admiral from the Navy. She developed the cobol computer language and was known as "the grand ole lady of software."

The tour spotlights the vital role of women in the Persian Gulf. There were over 35,000 military women, making up 6.6 percent of the 540,000 American troops who participated in Desert Storm. Women served in hundreds of jobs, enduring the same hardships and harsh conditions as their male counterparts.

Two women were killed in accidents during Desert Shield. Eleven women were killed during Desert Storm, of these 5 were killed in action. Following the cease fire, 2 women were killed in non-hostile accidents, for a total of 15 women who lost their lives.

Two of the 21 POWs were women. They were held captive and later returned to U.S. control. Another military woman was captured but she was returned to her unit, and not held by the Iraqi's.

Statistics on active duty women deployed in Desert Storm reveal the average age was 26 for enlisted, and 30 for officers. Many Desert Storm women in uniform were parents: * 2,467 single parent mothers. * 1,538 mothers married to a deployed service man. * 871 mothers married to non-deployed military man.* 2,719 mothers married to civilians. Total mothers deployed: 7,595.

MILITARY WOMEN'S CORRIDOR
This corridor points out the contribution of women
to the defense of our nation.

Prisoner of War/Missing In Action Corridor

This corridor is dedicated to all American Prisoners of War and Missing in Action from all wars. It is dedicated especially to the almost 2,500 Americans whose names are inscribed on the display who are still missing as a result of the Vietnam War. Visitors are requested to remain silent as they walk through this area, in honor of our POWs and MIAs.

At the end of the POW/MIA area there is an electronic eternal flame, lit by the Secretary of Defense in honor of these men and women and will continue to burn until the fullest possible accounting has been made.

Prisoner Of War Alcove

Most of the paintings in the Prisoner of War Alcove were done by civilian artist Maxine McCaffery. They include:

* **The Hanoi Hilton** – it was an actual POW camp. The names in the background are of actual POWs held there.
* **Colonel Fred V. Cherry** was one of the longest held POWs, held 7 1/2 years, he spent 702 days in solitary confinement. He was Hanoi's first black captive, tortured 93 days in a row. He is retired and lives in nearby Maryland.
* **Lt.General John P. Flynn** was the highest ranking officer held. It was kept secret so the North Vietnamese wouldn't know what a good thing they had. This made an early release possible. Afterwards, he returned to active duty and achieved the rank of 3-star general. He is now retired.
* **Colonel Edward L. Hubbard** was navigator on a recon mission on July 20, 1966. He was captured and held until 1973–seven years.
* **The 21 Desert Storm POWs** have received POW medals.

14

 # Getting Around

The Pentagon is well organized and well planned. The floor plan, which is identical for all five floors and the basement, resembles a giant cartwheel. Moreover, each floor is painted a different color and large signs are posted over doorways. The office numbering system is designed to identify the office easily by floor, ring and corridor. With a little experience, it becomes very easy to find any given destination.

How To Find Your Way Around
In The Pentagon

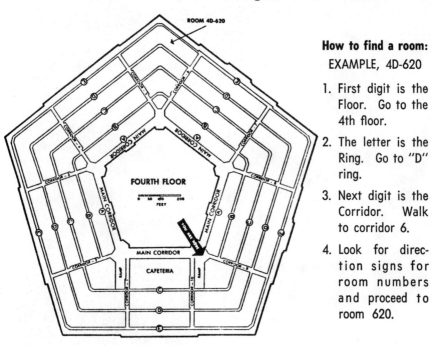

How to find a room:
EXAMPLE, 4D-620

1. First digit is the Floor. Go to the 4th floor.

2. The letter is the Ring. Go to "D" ring.

3. Next digit is the Corridor. Walk to corridor 6.

4. Look for direction signs for room numbers and proceed to room 620.

BUILDING FLOOR PLAN
Maps of the Pentagon are available at the Mall or River Entrances and the Concourse. Only the Concourse area is open to the public, except by escorted tour, or by personal escort of a Pentagon employee.

WWI Medal of Honor Ceremony, 24 April 1991

Constitution Corridor Dedicated

On September 15, 1987, Secretary of the Army John O. Marsh, Jr. dedicated the U.S. Constitution Soldier–Signers Corridor, as part of the military's observance of the 200th anniversary of the signing of America's historic governing Constitution.

Secretary Marsh noted the importance of America's uniformed service personnel: "I would hope that by speaking to you, representing each of your services, I might thereby speak to your service with thanks for the enormous contributions each of you makes to the defense of this country--recognizing that on September 17 we observe the 200th Anniversary of the signing of our great Constitution, and reminding ourselves that because of the service, and the sacrifice, of men and women who have worn the uniform you wear, we are able to commemorate that great event."

Lagoon

Nita Scoggan

MacArthur Corridor

This corridor honors General Douglas MacArthur's distinguished military career, which began when he graduated number one in his class at West Point. He served during 3 wars and under 9 Presidents during his 52 year military service. He and his father, Lt General Arthur MacArthur, are the only father–son to be awarded the Medal of Honor.

Excerpts from his famous speeches are on display, such as:

"A great nation which voluntarily enters upon war and does not see it through to victory must eventually suffer all the consequence of defeat. War's very object is victory, not prolonged indecision. In war, there can be no substitute for victory." Address to Congress 4/19/51

The Instrument of Surrender on display is one of three originals, one is in Japan, one is in the Archives in Washington, DC. The pen is one of six that were used in the signing of Japan's surrender.

At the surrender of Japan on September 2, 1945 the General said, "It is my earnest hope and indeed the hope of all mankind that from this solemn occasion a better world shall emerge...a world dedicated to the dignity of man and the fulfillment of his most cherished wish, of freedom, tolerance and justice...if we do not now devise some greater and more equitable system Armageddon will be at our door..."

"If the historian of the future shall deem my services worthy of some slight reference, it will be my hope that he mentions me...as that one whose sacred duty it became once the guns were silenced, to carry to the land of our vanquished foe the solace and hope and faith of Christian morals." Nat. Institute of Social Science 11/8/51

Secretary of Defense Caspar Weinberger cut the ribbon opening the corridor on September 10, 1981, stating: "We will shortly dedicate this corridor to the memory of General MacArthur...His memory will set an example, as did his actions in his life, to those who guard our shores and protect our liberties."

IF THE HISTORIAN OF THE FUTURE SHOULD
DEEM MY SERVICES WORTHY OF SOME SLIGHT MENTION,
IT WOULD BE MY WISH THAT HE RECORD ME NOT AS
A COMMANDER ENGAGED IN CONFLICTS AND CAMPAIGNS
EVEN THOUGH VICTORIOUS TO AMERICAN ARMS, BUT
RATHER AS ONE WHOSE HEART WAS IN THE RELEASE
ONCE THE GUNS WERE SILENCED AND THE CROSS OF THE LAND
OF OUR VANQUISHED FOES DEDICATED ITSELF IN ALL
FAITH OF CHRISTIAN MANHOOD TO THE SERVICE IN A
LINE A CENTURY HENCE CHILDREN IN THE CONSECRATION
TO THE ADVANCE OF PEACE, I WOULD REGARD A YIELD
EVERY HONOR WHICH HAS BEEN ACCORDED BY WAR.

Unusual Conveniences

The Pentagon offers unusual conveniences for its personnel, due to its isolated location. Shopping facilities, available on the 135 x 690 foot Concourse, are comparable to those of an average mall.

A book store, drug store, bank, Credit Union, barber and beauty shop, candy store, bakery, shoe repair and gift shop, an optometrist, Victorian boutique, computer software service, athletic shoe store, jewelry store, a mini branch of Woodies department store, a florist, post office, and a dry cleaners provide for the needs of the people. Other services, such as a travel agency is available on the Concourse. Truly, the Pentagon is a small city within itself.

Feeding the Pentagon population requires an immense food service operation. At wartime peak, daily consumption was 60,000 pounds of food. Approximately 17,500 meals are served daily in the six cafeterias, nine snack bars and dining rooms. There is seating for more than 4,000.

The stand–up snack bars fill nearly 30,000 orders daily, including 7,000 sandwiches, 30,000 cups of coffee plus thousands of cartons of milk and soft drinks. One cafeteria is open for breakfast, one snack bar operates from 7 a.m.–7 p.m. for the benefit of shift workers. An outdoor fast–food restaurant operates at lunchtime, in the 5–acre center court during warm weather months. Vending machines are located throughout the building.

A gymnasium is available on a membership basis, providing exercise equipment and facilities. Hundreds of joggers pound the pathways surrounding the Pentagon, to meet the physical requirements of the military.

A Prayer Room is open 24 hours a day so that personnel of any faith may come to pray and receive spiritual renewal and strength. A lovely stained glass window depicts the faith of our first President, the faithfulness of our Chaplains during WWII, and the importance of religious faith in our future. A Chaplain serving all faiths is here to counsel and pray with those who desire it.

The Mall Entrance
Pentagon Building

Nita Scoggan '81

Pentagon Pillars

Nita Scoggan

Unique Needs Met

There is a dispensary for military personnel, including physicians, dentists and nurses, providing routine medical and dental service, as well as emergency treatment when required. In addition, there is emergency care for civilian employees in need of first aid or treatment of illness during working hours.

The Army maintains a library for use by all Pentagon personnel, containing over 160,000 books, 230,000 periodicals and documents in various languages. Microfilm files are available to aid in research work.

The Pentagon operates its own electrical power plant, sewage treatment facility, heating and refrigeration plant. Electricity for the 70,000 building lights, ventilation, air conditioning, miscellaneous building equipment, and lighting for streets and parking areas is provided on the site.

Special communications requirements of the military services to reach installations, both continental and overseas locations, necessitates state-of-the-art equipment. Personnel are on duty 24-hours a day year-round, to maintain readiness.

To meet transportation needs, the parking areas cover 64 acres to accommodate approximately 10,000 cars. Two commercial parking lots offer parking for visitors, all other areas require permits. Nearby parking is designated for handicapped or van-pools. Outermost spaces, some 10 minutes walk from the Pentagon, go to 2-3 member carpools. The Pentagon Police check permits and violators are towed away and fined.

Taxis and bus terminals are located just outside the Pentagon. Many workers use the Metro, one of the newest subway systems in America, providing fast service to the Washington area.

There are many road signs, but no traffic lights and very few policemen, even at the height of rush hour. Even with the multitude of vehicles and pedestrians, the system works smoothly.

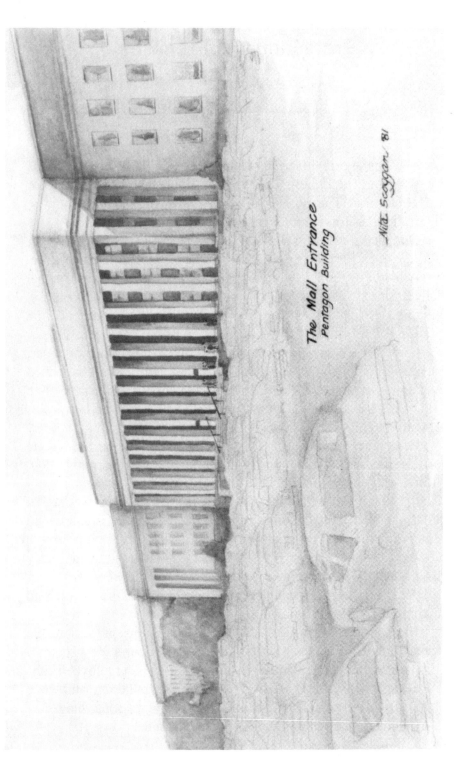

The Mall Entrance
Pentagon Building

Nita Scoggan '81

Mall Entrance

Nita Scoggan

Protecting the Premises

The Pentagon Police are on duty 24-hours a day. The guards are trained in fire fighting, and there is fire equipment on hand for immediate use. The police keep busy with military ceremonies, dignitaries, visitors, employees and occasional demonstrators.

No one is permitted inside the building without a badge or escort, except for the Concourse. Escorted weekday tours are free.

A patrol of the Pentagon is made by the United States Special Police. Checking for violations, such as people using an underpass, where pedestrians are not allowed; attempting to enter or leave the building by a freight loading platform and other Pentagon laws.

Once there was a murder victim found in the trunk of a car, parked in one of the Pentagon parking lots. "If that had happened over in town, it would have been forgotten," the Special Police said, "but because it happened in the Pentagon everybody still remembers it." The case was never solved.

Of course, there is crime. Cars in the parking areas are targets for thieves, and there are thefts within the building. Serious crime, such as espionage, is handled by the FBI.

In addition to the police, there are military guards on duty in certain restricted areas, and security-intelligence personnel who protect internal security matters.

People aren't the only visitors to the Pentagon. In the early 1950's, a duck, looking for a nesting spot, flew into the court yard, had her offsprings and settled down. Fish and Wildlife people had to come and carry them away.

Birds, mostly starlings, have found nesting places in the beautiful magnolia trees, used in landscaping around the structure. "Every evening, we get millions of starlings!" an employee said.

Occasionally, birds have gotten into the building, and have been difficult to remove. It seems there is always something new to challenge the Pentagon maintenance personnel.

River Entrance   Nita Scoggan

Pentagon Completed

On December 15, 1970, a small prayer room was dedicated. Secretary of Defense Melvin Laird felt the Pentagon was not complete without a place for employees to pray, if they so desired. As a former member of Congress, he was familiar with such a room located in the U.S. Capitol, for the purpose of prayer and meditation.

"In a sense, this ceremony marks the completion of the Pentagon," Secretary Laird said, "for until now this building lacked a place where man's inner spirit could find expression. In the Concourse and corridors of this building can be found a wide range of goods and services of a material nature, as well as places for work and duty.

Today, we are dedicating a room in the Pentagon as a place where the needs of the spirit–the needs of the inner man–can find satisfaction. It is a place where men and women can reflect and pray, and find guidance, as well as inspiration."

Secretary Laird continued, "The room offers a setting in which we can pray as we like. Its existence is a recognition of our dependence on God if we are to progress toward the peace which we seek for ourselves, and for all mankind. Peace is the business of this building–this small room is an affirmation of that."

The Secretary of Defense concluded, "Though we cling to the principle that church and state should be separate, we do not propose to separate man from God. For without Him, Who is the source of our being, the source of our wisdom, and the source of our strength, we can do nothing."

A Chaplain who serves all faiths is available to counsel and pray with anyone desiring it. Prayer and Bible study groups meet here before work or at lunch. Schedules for use of the small conference room is arranged through the Chaplain's office.

28

"Whom shall I send and who will go for us? . . .
Here am I: send me." Isaiah 6:8 *by Woodi Ishmael*

God Bless America

God bless America,
Land that I love,
Stand beside her—
And guide her—
Through the night with a light
from above;
From the mountains,
To the prairies—
To the oceans—
White with foam,
God bless America,
My home sweet home,
God bless America,
My home sweet home.

Statistical Tidbits

The Pentagon is one of the world's largest office buildings, on a total land area of 583 acres. It houses more than 24,000 people.

Cleaning the 83-acres of offices is accomplished at night–it is a gigantic job. About 100-acres of asphalt, and ceramic tile floor has to be kept scrubbed, waxed and buffed. The 7,748 windows must be cleaned. It was reported that more than 175,000 rolls of toilet paper, 35 million paper towels and 12,500 quarts of liquid hand soap were used annually, in cleaning the 280 restrooms.

Work crews constantly strive to keep the Pentagon and the 175-acre area neat and clean. Surrounding the building are 51/2 acres of sidewalks, and over 82 acres of roadways, which are cleaned with power equipment.

Interesting facts about the building:

Stairways 150
Escalators 19
Elevators 13
   Rest rooms 280
Fixtures 4,900
Drinking fountains 685
Electric clocks 4,200
   Light fixtures 65,000
Daily lamp replacements 1,000
Windows 7,748
Glass area . . . . 309,276 sq.ft.
   equals . . . . 7.1 acres
Parking space (acres) 67
Capacity (vehicles) 10,000
Office space (sq.ft.) 3,705,793

General Omar Bradley, Mrs. Mamie Eisenhower, and Secretary of Defense Melvin Laird at the dedication of the Eisenhower Corridor

The Pentagon Tour begins with a look at the importance of Security—as shown in this display of unique reminders. The author has loaned her private collection of security napkins distributed in the 1950's.

THE MILITARY WIFE

Poor girl never knows where on earth she's at,
'Cause home is wherever he parks his hat.
She packs up to move to hot plains of Nebraska;
Then orders are changed—and they go to Alaska.
She uncrates scarred furniture in snows or in rains,
And lays new linoleum between labor pains.
And during each move—I know it sounds strange,
The kids catch the mumps, or measles, or mange.

No time to get settled, she must dress up pretty,
And go to a party, be charming and witty.
She has to know contract, canasta, and chess,
And whether a straight or a flush is the best.
On a wide range of subjects, she has to discourse,
Must swim, ski and golf, and ride any old horse.
She must know all the songs, and traditions galore,
Memorize all the details of how HE won the war.
She quaffs all concoctions, from champagne to beer,
But not to extremes, lest she wreck his career.

He insists on economy, scans every check stub,
Yet the house must be run like a hotel or club,
Rooming and boarding any number of guests,
Eighteen or eighty, with pets that are pests.
She juggles the budget for his tropical worsted,
Though the seams of her only outfit have bursted.
When new uniform payments are finally arranged,
She learns to her horror that the dress codes have changed!
One year she has servants, and lives like a lady
The next does her own work while she has a new baby.
That there'll be a bank balance she has no assurance,
It all goes for sitters, or some kind of insurance.

At the age to retire, He is still hale and hearty,
Fit as a fiddle, the life of the party.
While she's old and haggard, all cranky and nervous,
Really a wreck from HIS twenty years service.
Retirement over, when all's said and done,
She tells everybody that the service life's fun!
She's loved every minute—why mercy! Good grief!
She'd be bored with a doctor, lawyer, or chief.

There's a big fancy medal—the service men wear it—
But it's wives who have earned it—the Legion of Merit.

Author unknown